FROM JAWS TO CLAWS

CHEETAH

Written by Eliza Nodes

Gareth Stevens
PUBLISHING

Published in 2026 by
Gareth Stevens Publishing
2544 Clinton St.
Buffalo, NY 14224

Written by: Eliza Nodes
Edited by: Rebecca Phillips-Bartlett
Designed by: Amelia Harris

All facts, statistics, web addresses, and URLs in this book were verified as valid and accurate at time of writing. No responsibility for any changes to external websites or references can be accepted by either the author or publisher.

Cataloging-in-Publication Data

Names: Nodes, Eliza.
Title: Cheetah / Eliza Nodes.
Description: Buffalo, NY : Gareth Stevens Publishing, 2026. | Series: From jaws to claws | Includes glossary and index.
Identifiers: ISBN 9781482475906 (pbk.) | ISBN 9781482475913 (library bound) | ISBN 9781482475920 (ebook)
Subjects: LCSH: Cheetah--Juvenile literature. | Cheetah--Life cycles--Juvenile literature.
Classification: LCC QL737.C23 N634 2026 | DDC 599.759--dc23

Printed in China

CPSIA compliance information: Batch #QW26GS:
For further information contact Greenhaven Publishing LLC at 1-844-317-7404.

Image Credits

Images courtesy of Shutterstock.com, unless otherwise stated.

Cover – Arturo de Frias, Efimova Anna, Chris Hill, Kwaczek. Recurring – Elena Pimukova, Impixmart, Nadya_Art, MrNoe. 2–3 – Nick Dale Photo. 4–5 – Gunter Nuyts, Stu Porter. 6–7 – Lucasdm, Efimova Anna. 8–9 – Breaking The Walls, Christian Musat. 10–11 – Mateo Juric, Bruce Crossey, Tartila. 12–13 – Nick Dale Photo, Dr Ajay Kumar Singh. 14–15 – imageBROKER.com, Kanale. 16–17 – Dr Ajay Kumar Singh, Sarah Maia Kerr. 18–19 – Wayne Marinovich, Heinz27. 20–21 – Mateo Juric, Valdecasas, Toseef Yousaf. 22–23 – GUDKOV ANDREY, EcoPrint, INDIGO MP Photography.

CONTENTS

WORDS THAT LOOK LIKE THIS CAN BE FOUND IN THE GLOSSARY ON PAGE 24.

The Cheetah

Cheetahs are known for their black spots and lightning speed. They mainly live in Africa. Their normal habitat is grasslands, but they will live anywhere that has a lot of food.

Female cheetahs usually live alone. Male cheetahs live in groups called coalitions. A coalition is made up of two or three brothers. This helps male cheetahs stay safe in the wild.

JAWS AND TEETH

Cheetahs are predators, which means they hunt prey to eat. Cheetahs have 30 teeth. The four longest teeth are called canines. Cheetahs' canines are much smaller than most other big cats' canines.

The cheetah's small teeth mean they eat small to medium sized animals. Their jaws are weaker than other big cats' jaws. This means it can take them a while to take down their prey.

EYES AND EARS

Cheetahs have golden or yellow eyes with black strips of fur underneath. It is thought that this black fur stops too much sunlight from getting in their eyes.

Cheetahs have small, round ears that turn toward any noise they hear. Their ears are not just used for hearing. They are also used for balance. This helps them make fast turns when running.

NOSE

Cheetahs have short noses but large nostrils. Large nostrils mean cheetahs can breathe in more oxygen. Getting plenty of oxygen is one of the things that helps cheetahs run so fast.

Humans usually take around 15 breaths a minute. When resting, cheetahs take 60 breaths a minute. When they run, this can go up to 150 breaths a minute.

A PURRFECT FACT

THE LONG, THICK HAIRS ON A CHEETAH'S FACE ARE CALLED WHISKERS.

VOICE

Many big cats, such as lions and tigers, roar. The cheetah is one of the few big cats that does not roar. Instead, cheetahs communicate with high-pitched chirping sounds.

A PURRFECT FACT

CHEETAHS CAN RECOGNIZE EACH OTHER FROM THEIR CHIRPS.

Cheetahs can make similar noises to house cats. They make a sound like a house cat's "meow." Purring is another sound cheetahs and house cats share. Purring usually means they are happy.

BODY AND FUR

Cheetahs can grow to around 5 feet (1.5 m) long. Their bendy backbones and long legs allow cheetahs to reach speeds of 70 miles (112 km) per hour. This makes cheetahs the fastest land animal.

A cheetah's fur is a gold color with solid black spots. Their fur camouflages them in long grass. This helps them to hide from predators and stay hidden when tracking prey.

CAN YOU SPOT THE CHEETAH IN THE LONG GRASS?

TAIL

A PURRFECT FACT
YOUNG CHEETAHS ARE CALLED CUBS.

Cheetahs have long tails that help them make quick turns when running. Female cheetahs use their tails to help their young follow them through long grass.

A cheetah's tail ends with a tuft of fur and a dark ring pattern. The rings and spots on each cheetah's fur are unique, just like your fingerprints.

LEGS

Cheetahs are amazingly fast, and this is because of their legs. Their long, slim legs mean each step they take is huge. A cheetah's single step can cover 23 feet (7 m).

A cheetah's legs and backbone are almost spring-like. This pushes their body forward as they run. This helps when they are chasing after prey.

PAWS AND CLAWS

Cheetahs' paw pads are tough and smaller than other big cats'. Smaller paws help cheetahs make sharp turns when running. Their paws barely touch the ground when running and chasing.

A cheetah's claws are blunt. They help the cheetah grip the ground when running. Their claws are not used to take down prey. Instead, cheetahs use their paws to trip up their prey.

A PURRFECT FACT

CHEETAH CLAWS ARE MADE OF KERATIN, JUST LIKE HUMAN FINGERNAILS.

LIFE CYCLE

Female cheetahs are pregnant for around three months. They usually give birth to two to six cubs. After 18 months, the cubs leave their mothers to look after themselves.

A PURRFECT FACT
LIFE CYCLES ARE THE STAGES LIVING THINGS GO THROUGH DURING THEIR LIVES.

Cheetah cubs have grey mantles down their backs. This is meant to copy a honey badger's back. Honey badgers are violent, and many predators avoid them. A cheetah cub's mantle protects them from predators.

GLOSSARY

CAMOUFLAGE to hide by blending into the surroundings

COMMUNICATE to pass information between two or more things

HABITAT a plant or animal's natural home

MANTLE area of long, differently colored fur

OXYGEN a natural gas that living things need in order to survive

PREGNANT when a female animal has one or more young or babies growing inside her

PREY animals that are hunted by other animals for food

UNIQUE one of a kind

VIOLENT willing to use force to physically hurt someone

INDEX